Challenges are Changes

You Live To Overcome

Blessing Chinemerem Agbakwuru

Copyright © Blessing Chinemerem Agbakwuru 2011

Challenges are Changes
You Live To Overcome

ISBN 978-0-9561824-1-8

Published in Great Britain by LanLegend Publishing

LanLegend
Publishing

52 Adelaide Road
LONDON E10 5NW
www.lanlegendpublishing.com

Author's cover photograph by Brownson Ifeanyi
Typeset and Cover by Marcellino Design
Printed by Lightning Source UK Ltd

📖

For my God-sent Daddy
Engineer Joshua N. Ahaiwe Jr.

DEDICATION

With love and humility, I dedicate this powerful book to God Almighty for helping me and giving me the grace to write it. I thank thee and praise thee, O thou God of my father, who hast given me wisdom and might, and hast made known unto me now what we desired of thee: for thou hast now made known unto us the King's matter. (Daniel 2:23)

📖

No one is born with a symbol of perfection

ACKNOWLEDGEMENTS

Since no person achieves success without the help and encouragement of others, I would be remiss if I did not acknowledge my debt by expressing my heartfelt appreciation to some very special people. These people have helped and encouraged me, and have worked hard for the achievement of my success.

Unfortunately, space will not allow me to list all the wonderful individuals I would like to include; so I humbly say to all of you whose names do not appear here, you have helped, inspired or befriended me, you know who you are; thanks!

Heading my list is my one and only Daddy from God, Engineer Joshua Nwanevunna Ahaiwe Jr., a God-sent man of integrity, honour, character and high esteem. His love, devotion and encouragement have made my life worth living and kept a spring in my gait. I thank you Daddy for being there for me from my childhood to date and for never saying no to any of my requests. You made a special statement that you want me to be far better than you and that by God's will; you will be there for me despite any odds. You said that as long as you are alive, you will share the list you have with me provided I need it and not just want it.

To my beloved parents - Mr. and Mrs. Chinyere Jeremiah Agbakwuru; who never rejected me or threw me away when I was born. I know I can count on your love even when I do not deserve it.

To most Reverends Chris Ekong and R.E.O. Iwuoha; who by their fatherly care have encouraged my life spiritually and supported my career financially.

It is my privilege to present Reverend C. Enyite, Reverend Ugochukwu Obi and Pastor Jarlath Onuegbu. These men of God have greatly blessed my life and their spiritual words have motivated me to manifest my potential. Also, through personal contact with them, my mind has opened up to some of the secrets that will bring solutions to my generation.

To Dr. Harrison Ugo Nwanjo; my favourite medical professor; who has been special to many people and who is a caring father.

My chance meeting on 4th Dec. 2010 brought me close to a caring mother - Mrs. Ijeoma Ejike, who by her intellectual and motherly instructions has kept the fire in me burning.

I respectfully recognise Ms Lanre Soyode; a successful author and publisher of books; for her help with editing and re-organising this book. Her devotion and love for me is something I must confess. May God reward her.

My thanks to thousands of people who God has used in my life as His practical instrument and those He is preparing to use in my life.

I remain indebted to my many close friends in the field of my study - the Medical Laboratory Science students of Imo State University of Nigeria; also, to my Church; the Lutheran Church of Nigeria and to the Nigeria Fellowship of Evangelical Students.

Finally, I am grateful to the IMSU Chapter and the National Fellowship of Christians of Medical Laboratory Science.

To all of you, thank you from the bottom of my heart.

TABLE OF CONTENTS

FOREWORD

On January 26th 1989, people witnessed something unusual in a village in Imo State of Nigeria. A baby girl with one leg was born into a poor family. She was their first child. This attracted crowds and gossip. The baby had no beauty to attract the nurses, doctors or people around. She was despised, looked down on and rejected by everyone. People imbibed the physical nature of what happened, but deep thinkers saw it as a blessing from God in a different way. This special baby was loved and cuddled by her sorrowful parents - as well as by me, Joshua. N. Ahaiwe Jr.

I, the undersigned, visited the hospital where she was born and I saw the beautiful girl born with one leg, sleeping calmly on a small bed. Her mother was seated on the same bed with tears rolling down her chin; her face down as if she had committed an atrocity and was ready to be killed by onlookers. But she did not know that God had blessed her with a special child.

After 7 months, I saw the child one day outside in the muddy rain. She could not crawl inside from the rain because her parents were not in. People around refused to take her into their homes. The child's mother realised her child was outside and ran home from the farm. She was filled with disgust and cried her heart out when she saw her helpless child in the rain with nobody around the place.

I monitored the growth of this child and observed some distinctive abilities in her. As such, I decided to give her all my love in my own little way. I decided to be there for her, having known that her biological parents might not be able to see her through any proper education. My reason was to help her to be the best possible to herself and not to be a public nuisance to any society she might find herself in. I wanted her to be a child and lady of good substance. By the grace of God, this child has turned out to be a first class academic material, a medical student and the best child among her equals in her community. She is also the inspirational writer of this book.

Time is a great healer and no person can fathom the mysteries of God. I pray to God to give me the grace to continue supporting her in my little way until she reaches the apogee of academics she desires. Her situation and what she is today explains that disability does not mean limitation. It also buttresses the saying that except in death, there is no limitation to success if one is recognised and genuinely supported.

Joshua N. Ahaiwe Jr.

INTRODUCTION

This book is the basic application to the facts of life and the keys to long living. There are three major things which surround man and stand as points to the challenges of life. These are fame, power and pleasure. It is in search of these things that man suffers and meets certain challenges. These challenges lead him to changes which influence his life positively.

This book will give you steps to take to overcome your challenges. It will also impact positive changes in your life. I am a physically-challenged person and I have been faced with different situations that have challenged my life. These have brought changes to my living. I wrote this book for the benefit of life. Life needs solutions to overcome challenges. Solutions will bring changes that will take you to a greater level.

As a growing child, I came across fellow physically-challenged people and youths with different problems and I made impact in their lives. I see myself as a solution and an encouragement to others. 'Challenges are Changes' will not only give you solutions to your life, it will also be an encouragement for you to live and overcome challenges.

I advise you to always read this book, for you do not know when you will take a mighty step to your greatness.

This is my first book. I need more encouragement and support from you. May the Almighty God bring changes in your life as soon as you desire.

You will never remain the same. Amen.

PART ONE

***

THE BEGINNING

CHAPTER ONE

❧❧

EARLY CHILDHOOD

I was born disabled on January 26th 1989 into a very wretched family with my father a drunk and my mother a petty trader in Imo State of Nigeria. With my disability, I suffered a lot of rejection which made me believe strongly in myself. I told myself that some day, I shall become a writer of books and even movies. Not only that, I believed I would become an actress and watch my own movies on my own television.

As I was saying all these things, I did not know the power of spoken words. I began to have inspirations and began to write. Sometimes I would give what I wrote to people to read in order to get inspired.

To date, I have written many documents and have read some of them in churches. In addition to this book, I have written a powerful script about my life titled 'Born to Be Great.' This script is still pending and has not been acted on because of sponsorship; but I trust in God that it will surely come to pass.

MY PARENTS

At 55 years of age, my father never knew a child would be born to him. He never thought of having a woman to call his wife. He just existed in this world for no good reason. Because of his alcoholic drinking, he was always questioning himself: 'Who will marry me and have me as a husband?' or 'Who will ever love me in spite of my predicaments and drinking habit?' But despite all odds, he got married to my lovely, calm mother and surprisingly, on one fateful Eke Market afternoon (the Igbo traditional market day); a baby's cry was heard under his roof. It was indeed a great day!

However, as much as he had longed to be a father, it was a physically-disabled child that was born to him and so; I was born to face a challenged life. My mother, Mrs. Josephine Ihuoma Agbakwuru was always there for me and never allowed me to feel bad, inferior or rejected about my condition. She never allowed me to go out begging for food, but worked hard both in the rainy and sunny seasons to make me feel like the other children in my family. She showed me love and care and assured me the best. Most especially, she remained thankful to God for giving me to her despite my physical disability.

As a physically-challenged person, I strongly believe in what I can do and what God can do through me to influence my generation. 'Challenges, I know too well, are changes which I must live to overcome.'

Because of my condition as a physically-challenged child, I spent two years crawling. I found it very difficult to walk and didn't walk until after the age of two. My mother had to go to the market very early in the morning for her sales whilst carrying me around on her back. One day to her greatest surprise, I began to walk. God's hands had lifted me up!

As soon as I began to walk, I started disturbing my parents to take me to school. With my own way of walking, I started nursery school when my mates were still at home. I was a wonder to many because God Almighty had been, and continues to be my strength. Nobody can fathom God's mystery.

My poor parents and I lived in an old dingy hut, roofed with papers and plastic. It had one room and we shared one bed. There was no ceiling, no proper floors and it had very little ventilation. There was no electricity and no television. It was in this room that we received visitors, kept our food utensils and our clothes. It was also in this room that my father usually fought with my mother. We had no toilet. The one my father tried to create was closed by family out of hatred.

As a child, I did virtually what every child did for their parents. I followed my parents to the farm and cultivated with them. I managed to fetch water with my mother's old bicycle even when I could not ride it properly. I prepared meals the way my mother taught me, washed our clothes, fetched firewood from the bush, etc. I did these things to make my parents happy and to put smiles on their faces.

Life was really sweet and awful - sweet because even in my condition, I enjoyed every aspect of help I rendered to my poor parents, but awful because my parents were not meeting up with my needs as their only child.

It was at this time that I began to have goals, dreams and ambitions to meet up with my challenges. I began to discover my talents which included writing. At the age of ten, while I was in primary six, I was able to connect electricity into our house using an ordinary battery, stick, wire and light bulb.

The most painful part of my experiences was that my father, after drinking alcohol in the bar, would return home and start to beat my mother. This would be the time when my mother had just come back from the market; when she would have prepared a meal without fish or meat and this would annoy my father so much that he would start fighting her. This hurt me a lot and fellow children mocked me over these acts between my parents. They also teased me over my father's drinking behaviour and I dropped out of school because my parents could not afford my fees.

Each time I went to the market with my mother, I kept remembering my dreams and visions and what I wanted to become in life. Tears would roll down my cheeks as I wondered how I could possibly accomplish my dreams in the market. I wondered how my dreams could ever come true after dropping out of school. But I did not let my mother know what was going on in my mind so that she would not feel bad and start crying too.

At the age of six whilst in primary three, I got my first mobility aid through the tremendous help of Akpodim Rehabilitation Centre at the Orthopedic Hospital, Uturu Okigwe in Abia State. This mobility aid was an artificial limb, meant to be changed three years after outgrowing it.

At the age of nine, again, I got my second walking aid through them. It was after this period that the Akpodim Centre stopped functioning and stopped sponsoring me. What a world of pain! Then, after three years of outgrowing the limb; when I was 12 years old in secondary school; I began to write letters to various people for help. But nothing came from any of them.

Life was so awful that my parents could not afford my school textbooks and exercise books. However, I was very brilliant; and each term I came first in class, I had to go to people with my result, pleading with them to kindly give me money to buy books. After realising I couldn't continue with this,

I started going inside the bush on weekends to pick palm kernels. These I would crack and sell to raise money to buy my books. I also used some of the money to buy clothes, soap, cream and other essential personal items for myself. I remember several times getting wounded inside the bush and having to be treated by the chemist in my village. It was very hard doing all of this, not minding my condition as a physically-challenged person.

At Christmas, I used to feel rejected because I knew my parents could not afford to buy me lovely clothes and I could not quarrel with them for being poor. However, I felt unhappy and cheated each time I saw fellow children dressed nicely in fanciful outfits and wearing good shoes during this festive season.

The situation got so critical that I stopped going to secondary school in my fourth year and instead, started helping my mother in the market. Very early in the morning, I would set out with my mother for the 100km trip to the market and would stay the whole day with nothing to eat. Sometimes my mother would feel so concerned about me that she would cry, especially when she saw my fellow students in their uniform, coming at lunch time to buy things from the market.

But I would encourage her not to bother; that I would finish my studies, write my exams successfully and go on to university. I told her that I would be great and become an encouragement to my generation.

One day, somebody came up to me and told me that he would be there for me by God's will. I saw him as God-sent. His name was Engr. Joshua Ahaiwe Jr. and he was visiting home from abroad. He told me he would help me to become even better than himself. I have referred to him as 'My Daddy' throughout this book.

He transformed and overhauled my wrecked life and showed me the fatherly care I had been longing for. He promised to help me change my walking limb before he travelled back.

Unfortunately, due to unforeseen circumstances, he was not able to help me as promised. But I knew he had me in mind.

After some time, I heard that he lost his job and his life was messed up by some of his family members. As a result he ran into financial difficulties.

I remember when I was walking with him inside his compound; he set three mathematical questions before me, of which I was able to answer two. He said to me, 'By God's grace, I will take you to any height regarding your academics.'

I began to experience the most difficult part of life at this time. Sometimes, as I walked down the road or headed for school, I would give vent to my emotions. Feelings of fear would run through my nerves as I wondered if my artificial limb would pull off and disgrace me. I decided to always have a needle, some thread, a few small nails and a rock in my pocket to enable me repair my limb if it got spoilt on the way. At a point, I padded the limb to meet up with the height of my right leg and decided to walk erect.

As I was passing through these tough experiences, I was also busy looking for sponsorship of N150,000 to get a new limb. But I could not find any help; definitely not from my family because at this time, there was a row in their midst. My biological father was busy with his hobby of drinking and could do nothing to help me. It was very terrible indeed.

There was absolutely no one to run to for help and it was at this point that my sweet mother decided to divorce my father. She thought of his alcohol drinking, her suffering as he frequently beat her and the family's hatred towards us. She was determined to divorce him. But she wondered where she would take me and what my father's fate would be if she left. Her parents were dead and her siblings were too poor to take on any additional responsibility. I advised my mother against divorcing. I told her that since we had already coped with the suffering, we needed to continue having faith, till things got better.

But my father's behaviour towards us did not get better. It was uncontrollable. Sometimes, after drinking alcohol, he would be at the roadside molesting everybody passing him by. He made us a laughing stock and put shame on our faces. Sometimes, as I came back from school with fellow pupils, I would see my father by the roadside, drunk to stupor, unable to control himself. This usually prompted the pupils to mock me and tell me all sorts of things. Then, I would start crying all the way to meet my mother in the market and tell her how my father had disgraced me.

But I was sure something must have prompted my father to behave the way he did. He must have been frustrated and must have had some terrible experiences.

CHAPTER TWO

෩෬

MY FATHER'S STORY

My father was crying bitterly as he told me his story:

'My daughter,' he started, 'I have passed through hell and come back. I was rejected, hated and discriminated against among my fellows. My father married three wives and my mother was the third and youngest. My mother was respectful, caring and loving to be with, but she began to experience hatred and rejection and was treated as an outcast immediately she gave birth to me. No one believed she could give birth. I was intelligent but there was no one to send me to school. My father was willing to help me before his death - he was a very old man when he died. My step-siblings hated both me and my mother. They never included us in their plans as one family. The same hatred they had for my mother was automatically transferred to me - even to date. They made me suffer all kinds of sicknesses just to see me dead. My mother carried me on her back to look for places where I could be healed. When I became well, I helped her on the farm to enable us eat. My mother was happy to see me alive - she did not care if I was useful to her or not, she only wanted to see me alive. I had no friends, no full-blooded brothers or sisters and no one to cheer me up or encourage me in life. There was nothing to make me happy and nothing to make my life meaningful.

Then, I began to smoke and drink. At a point, I decided to stop smoking but I still drank. Every effort I made to become someone in life failed. I decided not to get married because I did not think anyone would want to marry me. But today, it's a dream come true that I have a child like you. Truly, God gave you to me to dry my tears; to restore me and help me achieve all I thought I could not achieve. May God bless you and provide you with helpers.' My father concluded his story.

This story I kept in my heart till today.

CHAPTER THREE

෨ා෬

THE FOOD I ATE

It is not funny to say here that as a child, I never ate a good, nourished or balanced diet. Among the six basic classes of food, my mother always prepared those high in carbohydrates which are the most affordable in Nigeria - especially amongst the poor. My mother could afford this because she was the breadwinner of the family. However, this was not to say that my father did not make a 'little' contribution towards the upkeep of the house. Even with his drinking habit, he made sure he purchased a few things from what he earned as a native doctor and peasant farmer.

As a matter of fact, there was no specific meal for breakfast, lunch or dinner. Any food was served at any time. Life was so tough that several times, my lovely parents and I starved - especially when my mother did not make any sales in the market. As a consequence, I starved virtually every day and was lucky just to have something light for breakfast. Most times, I was irritated and tired of eating carbohydrates all the time, particularly when I saw other children eating nourishing foods rich in protein and vitamins.

In spite of this, my mother always did something to make me happy; she made sure she brought home my favourite meal (tea and bread) each time she made good sales from the market as a petty trader. My happiness was always her concern.

Because I understood the condition of my family as a child, I never for one day condemned my mother's food; rather, I would praise her as much as possible and tell her how delicious it was. I knew very well that someday, everything would be fine. I had to remember the saying that, 'the survival of a man does not depend on his fitness' and that background is not the only answer to survival. For this reason, I kept my fingers crossed, watching and hoping in God.

CHAPTER FOUR

ဆဲလ

GROWING UP A TEENAGER

I was 14 years old when I began to read the Igbo bible in my church. My father never taught me neither did my mother. The truth of the matter was that my father did not attend church nor was my mother strong in the things of God, but I took it upon myself even as a youngster, to know God and serve Him. Many parents became influenced by this and were encouraged to teach their children how to read the bible. As a matter of fact, I usually represented my church in bible quizzes and other important activities.

Because I love education and strongly believe it as the only way to success and key to greatness, I had a burning desire to go school. I wanted to become somebody in life so that even if I never got married, I would at least feed myself.

I became a celebrity when I came first in my class during my first year at secondary school. This news got to my primary school teacher, Mr. Godwin Madugba, and also to my late pastor who cheered me up and made me feel happy. My biological father could not do anything for me. I grew up having God in my mind and I had a burning desire to achieve my powerful goals in life. My dream was that I must go to school and become a medical doctor. I kept remembering that: 'A desire to achieve is better than a dream without vision.'

Throughout primary school, I was known as a brilliant student and when I got to secondary school, it was the same.

You are at your best when you operate to the standard of your potential.

CHAPTER FIVE

৪১৫৪

TOUGH TIMES

Life got tougher when my grandmother died. My parents and I were still living in the same old dingy hut, roofed with lots of paper and plastic. It happened that the house began to collapse and there was no one to run to for help. It was indeed a raw deal.

At this point, the idea of 'Challenges are Changes - I must live to overcome' came into my head. It was on 14th December 2005 when my grandmother died and I ruminated on what to do to make sure she had a proper burial. I also wondered what to do to stop our only house from collapsing, but there was nothing I could do and no one to turn to for help. When it rained, it rained heavily and the sun scorched us. It was as if there was no hope. My father managed to cover the house with nylon but still, I could not bear it.

Life continued this way until one day in one of my quiet moments, I had an inspiration to write a letter to one man in my village whom I had often heard of but never knew. His name was Mr. Chimah Ihekoromba. I wrote a letter to him telling him about the condition of our collapsing house and pleaded with him to help us build a new one. As a matter of fact, I wrote this letter without the consent of my parents and sent it through Mr. Christopher Mmezi. Two days later Mr. Chimah Ihekoromba sent a reply thanking the person that wrote the letter. He ordered our house to be rebuilt two weeks before the burial of my grandmother which was on 31st December 2005.

The burial was sponsored by Hon. Independence Ogunewe who gave my father N50,000.

However, it was during the time of rebuilding the house that it was made known to my parents the secret behind the new house. This made my father grateful towards me although he didn't express his love for me. My mother was very grateful to have me as a child. In the end, the house with three rooms was rebuilt for us all. There was so much joy!

My father had another wife who gave birth to a little boy, but this woman acted strangely by refusing to breastfeed her new-born baby. As an only child of my mother, I found myself loving my step-brother very much and I felt sorry that his mother refused to give him any breast milk. He was always happy whenever I came back from school to stay with him. He was a very smart and intelligent boy and I called him 'my love.'

At the age of 17, it was time to write my W.A.E.C exams and I sought for help, but could not find any. One day, I took a bold step to meet Hon. Bennett Nwamuo; the proprietor of Model Secondary School, Amumara. I expressed my deep feelings and pleaded with him to help me so I could write my W.A.E.C exams in his school. There were tears rolling down my cheeks and the man was so touched by my story that without hesitation, he registered me for free at his school to write the exams. After the W.A.E.C exams, I was the only science student out of 69 that made my nine papers.

It was after my W.A.E.C exams that I came across a guy named Kingsley from Rivers State of Nigeria who had recently had an accident whereby one of his legs was cut off. He was shocked when he saw me and I was also shocked when I saw his condition.

'What happened to you?' He asked, looking surprised.

'What happened to you?' I asked back.
He explained to me how he had the accident.

'So sorry, it's quite a pity; but mine is natural.' I told him. 'I was born to be great.'

Days later, he helped me by taking me to the 'Free Artificial Walking Limb' sponsored by the Indian Community in Anambra State of Nigeria. Since then, they started sponsoring my limb.

CHAPTER SIX

❧❦❧

FINISHING W.A.E.C EXAMS

After getting my limb and finishing with my W.A.E.C exams, I had nowhere to go and spend my holidays. As I mentioned earlier, my father was the only child of his mother and his father had married three wives. Those other wives did not like my father so I could not go and stay with them. My mother's own family was poor and this meant I could not go there either.

Later, my church; the Lutheran Church of Nigeria, Akpodim; sent me on a computer training course. After this, I managed to write my first JAMB (Joint Admission Matriculation Board) exams for a university career. But I had nobody in mind to sponsor me.

My friends and everyone who knew I was writing the university JAMB exams asked me: 'Chinemerem, who will sponsor you? Your father is a drunk and your mother is a petty trader; who is going to sponsor you?'

'God will train me.' I answered. But I missed getting an admission that year. However, I was courageous to write the exam the following year and this time, I scored well. But I still wondered who would sponsor me.

Sitting alone on that dingy seat, ruminating deeply over my life with tears rolling down my cheeks, I kept wondering: 'Who will sponsor me at the university?' I knew only God Almighty could help me. So, one fateful morning, I heard the news that the man I call 'My Daddy' - Engr. Joshua Ahaiwe Jr., was back in the village.

I was so excited that I ran to his father's compound to see him and lo and behold, I saw him for the second time in my life. He hugged me like a father who had missed his child for a long time.

'How did you get your walking limb?' He asked, remembering how he was unable to help me the last time.

'It's a long story.' I said as I put my credentials in his hand. He looked through and was very excited.

'You want to be a medical doctor; are you sure you can make it?'

'Yes Daddy I can, by the grace of God.'

'I am going to make sure that you study Medicine & Surgery at the university and become a medical doctor.' He assured me.

When he returned overseas and heard that my medical admission was taken from me and given to a rich man's child, he spent well over half a million Naira (Nigerian money) to get the admission back. It did not work straight away, but eventually, God made it happen through him. To that, I said: We are all God's workmanship and blessed to be a blessing to others. Thank you God in your citadel.

At this point of my life when 'My Daddy' came into my life again, I really began to know what happiness was. He assured me that by God's will and as long as he was alive, he would be there for me. He took me up again as his own child and paid a huge sum of money to secure my admission into university. He promised to be there for me in difficulty and happiness. Then I said to myself: 'Finally, I am going to university!' I was so happy that tears of joy rolled down my cheeks. What a world made so beautiful indeed!

CHAPTER SEVEN

❧❧❧

LIFE AT UNIVERSITY

When I newly came into university, it was like a new world altogether. I could feel all eyes on me; some students looked at me strangely, some rejected me while others tried to encourage me. I saw all of this as a big challenge that I must overcome. With my disability, I had to make sure I was seated in the lecture hall by 7 am every morning, waiting for the lecturer and other students to arrive. The most challenging part of it was that I walked to school every day and if I missed being in the lecture hall by 7 am, there would be no seat for me. I therefore had to make a few friends who helped me secure a seat whenever I could not make school early. Also, it was obvious that I must live in a hostel. I resumed the campus late and almost all hostels were full, but I was lucky enough to get somewhere cheap.

During my early stay in the hostel, I contracted a disease I never thought would be healed. I cried each time I looked at my body and saw the disease. This continued until one day I bought an antibacterial cream and miraculously, the infection disappeared. I was still living in the hostel and could not complain about it to my biological father because I was afraid. I was praying to God to make a way for me.

In the hostel, most of the students were children of rich parents. It was terrible living in the midst of those with such wonderful backgrounds whose parents were commissioners, doctors, lecturers, managers, etc. These students were comfortable because their parents provided everything they needed. They had good clothes, beautiful shoes, well-maintained hair and they looked attractive. They had beautiful mobile handsets that contained music, camera, recording functions and browsing facilities. They had beautiful beds with comfortable mattresses. They never lacked anything; they had weekly pocket money and owned good cooking utensils. They used sanitary towels but I could only afford to use tissue paper. This truly took me to another dimension of challenges.

The mobile handset I was using had lasted three years and the worst part of it was that it had no music, camera or browsing functions. I can recollect one fateful evening as I read in my room, my roommates were playing music from their phones and a friend of theirs walked into the room. She looked around, surprised, and then asked me, 'Chinemerem, where is your own music?' I managed to smile but could not answer her question. I knew she would not ask me for my own fan because each of my roommates had a fan. I also knew she would not ask me for my own radio, television or laptop because again, both of my roommates had these things. But I'm sure she was touched by the unfairness of the environment. What a world!

Whenever my roommates ate delicious meals, I could only have garri in water without milk or sugar. Sometimes, I would drink water throughout the whole day, and even in this condition, I was the breadwinner of my family. When these rich and privileged girls were thinking about their enjoyable lifestyles, I was busy thinking about my condition, my family and how to achieve a fulfilling career.

The truth of the matter was that the little money 'My daddy' sent me for my school fees and provisions was split in two. I gave half of it to my parents so that they could eat at least once a day and take care of my only brother. This sometimes caused me to starve and faint in school.

As a matter of fact, I found it very difficult to buy textbooks that were recommended, such as the 'medical dictionary' and medical equipments for my practical classes. As medical students, we were meant to adhere to a professional dress code every day but unfortunately, I found that I could not afford it because it was very costly. I only managed to wear one dress which I had sewn for a long time.

Sometimes, I was forced to borrow books from friends but the books never lasted long with me because the girls soon wanted their books back. Sometimes, when we were given assignments which involved browsing the internet, I felt my fellow mates hated me because I had neither a laptop nor the huge amount of money to pay for one. When I tried to borrow a laptop from them, they would give me a condition that I must help them with their own assignment first, before doing my own.

Sometimes, I had to borrow money from my roommates to eat. Many of the clothes I wore and handbags I used were passed down to me by my loved ones. Clothes were so costly that I could not afford to buy good ones. If I managed to buy any clothes, I would pay half of the money and owe the seller the rest, promising to pay the balance whenever God provided it for me.

My stay at the hostel changed when 'My Daddy', Engr. Joshua Ahaiwe Jr., came back home and I went to meet him at the hotel where he lodged. On reaching there, I met a fellow student having a chat with him and luckily, this student was bold enough to tell him how bad my hostel was.

The student recommended that I move from there to a better place and although it would cost more, 'My Daddy' did not mind the extra cost. That was how I was able to move to a better accommodation.

'My Daddy' made me proud the day he walked hand in hand with me on the street. People were looking at us and a man walked up and asked. 'Is she your child?'

'Yes, she is.' Replied 'My Daddy'.

The man said he loved the way 'My Daddy' held my hand and carried my school bag whilst walking according to my ability and strength.

I thank you Almighty God. You are my all and everything.

CHAPTER EIGHT

HOPE FOR THE FUTURE

Right now, my step-brother has become my top priority. He is a sweet and loving boy, I love him so much and he loves me too. Truly speaking, I cannot afford to see him suffer or be deprived of anything. He is now four years old and I have decided to use some of the money 'My Daddy' sends me to help my little brother start nursery school. I have paid his school fees, bought him a uniform, some exercise books, shoes and a school bag.

Last year, in March of 2010, his mother (my step-mother), gave birth to beautiful twin girls and again, refused to breast-feed them. I was not happy.

I know I will influence my generation positively and contribute good values to their lives. I strongly believe that the right time has come for my generation including the physically-challenged, to rise and shine. This is the time for them to maximise their potential and become great in life.

For the sake of my siblings, I recently joined a non-governmental organisation called the Niger Delta Care which was set up for the benefit of vulnerable children, orphans and physically-challenged people. My family encouraged me to be a volunteer and I was made coordinator of around 150 children who are either disabled or living miserable lives in the villages.

Because I understand the sufferings and needs of these children, I have volunteered to seek help on their behalf to enable them cope with their everyday challenges. I have several files including that of an 8-year old girl who was born paralysed with her spinal cord outside her body - a bit above her hip. Her father is dead and her mother is a peasant farmer who carries the child on her back wherever she goes. This child needs education, a wheelchair, clothing, feeding and so on. My own situation has made me search for these kids because I feel great sympathy for them; even though I am also in need of help.

As a medical student with a burning desire to progress, I hope to become a medical laboratory scientist after my graduation. I also have a vision to be the first female governor of my state.

PART TWO

***

CHALLENGES ARE CHANGES YOU LIVE TO OVERCOME

CHAPTER NINE

෨෧෪

THE FATE BEYOND DISABILITY

It is right to state that challenges are the key to observing changes in the life of every individual. When you are challenged socially, financially, emotionally or spiritually, you think of ideas. Bring that which is in you and make great changes.

Ignorantly, the world's point of view on disability is that disability is the worst thing that can happen to anybody. But the fact is that physical challenges have no effect on whatever gifts or potential God has deposited in you. Nobody is an accident into this world. If you think you are of life's challenges, you have reason to give.

In my daily life as a growing young lady, blessed greatly but physically-challenged, I found life 'complex' and 'simple'. Complex because my artificial left leg cannot do all that my right leg does and simple because I came to realise who I am; that I am great, different, gifted and special - moreover, there cannot be any other me (Chinemerem) in the whole universe. What about you? To live beyond the fate of my disability, I found myself worthy of esteem. I also found myself very important and strong. 'I am fearfully and wonderfully made.' (Psalm 139:14).

I am the best that God created. My condition as a physically-challenged person is not one that I love or cherish. It is not what anyone should desire because when you are challenged, you are exposed; but this brings you quick solutions. Souls will be touched for your sake and God's favour will follow you. It is not a thing of joy to be physically-challenged, but remember that: 'You are made for the works of God to be made manifest in you.' (John 9:3)

Sometimes, I think of the time, i.e. seconds, minutes, hours, days and even months that God devoted to making me in this fearful and wonderful way. Do you know that in spite of life's odds, God did not create us to suffer, cry, or feel rejected in life? God said: 'Before I formed you in the belly I knew you and before you came out of the womb, I sanctified you.' (Jer.1:5)

God wants you to stop feeling bad about your life and your present situations and recognise your potential. Remember that, 'You are at your best when you operate to the standard of your potential.' God wants you to pick courage and wax strong in your spirit; to be filled with wisdom to face life and its challenges. God wants you to live for Him and live beyond the fate of your challenges. So, know who and whose you are, and let who you are be made known to the world. Moreover, let your potential be manifested as you live to the fulfilment of your dreams. A desire to achieve is better than a dream without vision. One philosopher claimed that: 'As many as 150 wrinkles appear on your face when tensed, contrary to 15 that will appear on your face when cheerful.'

So, living a life of inferiority, anger, rejection, frustration and worry can never help you recognise who you are or how to make positive changes in your life. Why worry?

The difficult situation of my disability has guaranteed me the courage and zeal to move ahead into prosperity and greatness in Christ Jesus. This has changed my life positively. I am great, gifted, different and special! What about you? I strongly believe in what I can do and what God can do through me to influence my generation. What about you? Think of your life today and live to overcome your challenges.

Every man is disabled in certain ways whether physically or not. No man is born with a symbol of perfection. If you think you are free of life's challenges, you have reasons to give. As you have disabilities, so also do you have abilities.

We are disabled! Yes, you are! I am! But in all, let's appreciate God who made life to be. He watches over us. Just be YOURSELF!

Morals

God is the giver of children. You cannot live unless you are born, you cannot be born unless you are conceived and you cannot be conceived unless both parents are productive. Think about it.

Please dear parents, any child you bring forth into the world shows that you are productive and fruitful. As a physically-challenged child, I advise you my dear parents to joyfully, happily and gladly appreciate any child God has given you; whether physically-challenged or not. Learn to be grateful to God and to your fellow human beings.

To you my fellow physically-challenged friends remember that there is something in you that makes you the person you are. You are not an accident into this world. As the day gives birth to another day by passing through the night, so also will your dreams give birth to achievement by passing through determination. So maximise your potential and live great. Live beyond pity!

Prayer

May the challenges you are passing through now bring positive changes in your life and may you live beyond the fate of any disability or challenges you will encounter in life. Amen! Please, always remember that there is God who is our Father who cares for us.

CHAPTER TEN

ඐ

THE HUMAN HUMOUR

Days of life are vanity of vanities where man strives for the flesh. Sometimes I think I inhabit the part of life where life is miserable and awful.

Every good work of man is surrounded by atoms of tongues and an unbearable break of mouth where man encounters difficulties. Sometimes I say man should prepare himself for the coming of tomorrow for it comes speedily; but when troubles arise, it passes slowly. This is the situation of life. Life is like a good seed planted in the garden and covered with a heap of sand. As the seed germinates from the ground, so also shall every buried soul arise from the dead on the day of resurrection. So be wise in your actions and fully put your trust in God.

In my quiet moment as a scholar, I asked myself: 'Who is saved from the difficulties, pains, sorrows and afflictions of life?' Then I recalled the saying: 'When there is a will, there is a way.'

So reach out for the valuables of life that will enlighten your horizon, for without these, life is empty. Just trust in God. Give your life to Him and you will be saved.

Sometimes I would ask myself: who will love me and cherish me as a physically-challenged person? Then I would remember that God is my helper and He cares for me. I love God who made the world and the life in it. Charles Swindon said, 'The longer I live, the more I realise the impact of life.'

Attitude to me is more important than the past, education, money, circumstances or what people think, say or do. I am convinced that life is 10 percent of what happens to me and 90 percent of how I react to it. Stop musing over the present situation of life and make a better future. Forget about limitations and operate on a new state and a new day, for life is empty. Life is full of mysteries and wonders but God is the ultimate of life. Sometimes, when I consider the handiworks of God, i.e. human beings of different shapes and attitudes, I ask myself: who is free from the problems of this empty world?

Life is a place of study: it has its books and it teaches its lessons. Impressions come with inspirations, ideas come with solutions. Sometimes I would ask: 'Who is he in this world to console me over my feelings except God? Sometimes I would give vent to my emotions, knowing very well that we are uniquely created as human beings for a unique purpose. We are created to carry out certain things that other creatures cannot do.

You cannot be yourself until you deposit that which is in you, i.e., your potential and skills. You're never born empty. This is a wanton world. God gives life and he owns the world and every atom of things in it. I am fully optimistic that a mass of people live lives of quietness, regret, and confusion where they do not understand the secrets of life. This is a world of attachment; a world of management and a world of limits, but there is no limit to your potential. Your gifts can take you anywhere except to the limit you create yourself. Sometimes when I feel everything has ended, I encourage myself by strongly believing in what I can do and what God can do through me. Sometimes I ask: Who is good? Who is perfect? Who is righteous?

Let your good deeds overcome your bad ones and you will be great with the insurance of life. The only easy way of life is 'money' - I mean righteous money.

Money is a minor substance without which life is lost. Money is paper valued in a special way by people; without it, life is crude. Sometimes I wonder why this common paper of currency should be a hold-up of life. I believe that life is true living; that we should live to please Him who owns it. We should also stick to the fact that: 'Challenges make man strong in the spirit whilst making him believe there is God.'

No matter the difficulties of life, with endurance and faith in God, we will overcome and become that which God has purposefully made us to be.

Remember: 'Your destiny lies in your hand so let it die or make it live. Live to overcome before you die!'

CHAPTER ELEVEN

❧❧

GOD'S PARENTAL CARE
TO HIS CHILDREN

As a scholar, I would like to relate these qualities of God as a father who has intensive care for His children. In four senses, I like to describe God as a caring father, the creator of Israel, father of Jesus and father of believers. God is also the father of mankind. This is revealed in the scriptures.

Instances

Paul said in Acts 17:28-29, that we are the offspring of God. In Luke 3:38, he said that we are the sons of God by origin. Genesis 3:8 said: He is God and father. Isaiah 63:16 reads: Doubtless you are father, though Abraham was ignorant of us and Isaac does not acknowledge us. You O Lord are our father; our redeemer from everlasting is your name.

The prophet Isaiah reveals that God is father. Jesus himself who referred to God as father said in Matthew 23:9: We call no man on earth father for we have one father who is in heaven.

By this, Jesus wanted to enforce the father Lord in the minds of the people.

There are also many scriptures that reveal and confirm the father as Lord. As a father, God takes full responsibility of taking care of his children including other living creatures that exist upon the earth. See God's caring ability in Psalm 145:15 - The eyes of all look expectantly to you and give them their food in due season. You open your hand and satisfy the desire of every living thing.

Food supply

We know that one of the duties of parents is to make sure that the child does not go hungry no matter the condition of the country's economy. The father makes sure that there is food on the table on a daily basis because food is important if growth must take place. The Bible says that God is a father because He supplies food for both human beings and other creatures. It also says that God is a father because He satisfies the other needs of man such as clothing. In Genesis 3:2, God used the skin of animals to cover the nakedness of Adam and Eve, and even though they disobeyed Him, as a father, it was His responsibility to cover the nakedness of His children.

In Deuteronomy 8:4, the bible records that the garments of the people did not wear out and their feet did not swell for forty years. God preserved them for forty years in the wilderness.

Also in Exodus 16:12-14, God gave the people of Israel bread and meat. This also reveals that God knows what is good for His children as the earthly father does. So God as a father is committed to supplying us all things that make up our well-being. God is concerned about our cleanliness, both inside and outside. In 2 Corinthians 6:4-18, God promised to be a God and a father if only we will separate ourselves from such things that defy the spirit and body because He is a holy father that repels every evil act.

David said in Psalm 27:10: 'When my father and mother forsake me, then God will take care of me.' This scripture reveals whatever our earthly father and mother can do for us but God does it better and perfect. One major quality about God is that He cannot fail. He's always faithful unlike our earthly fathers who do fail time without number. God is ever trust-worthy and diligent in keeping to His promises of fatherhood to us. Jesus Christ confirms this in Matthew 6:9-13 and 6:30-34 where he admonished his disciples to pray to God for daily bread and protection from evil. We need to ask ourselves if we are good godly parents. Our children learn more from watching us than direct teaching. So we must be careful about what we say and do. Proverbs 19:18 says: Discipline your children while there is hope. If you don't, you will ruin their lives. Children who grow up undisciplined feel unwanted and unworthy. They will also lack direction and will rebel as they get older. They will have no respect for authority or God. Discipline should be a balance of love because God realises that discipline is painful. I also believe that it's important to involve your children in the church and ministry when they are young. Introducing a bible-based church to your children will teach them how to study the word. You can discuss what's going on in their lives and relate to them the stories of the Bible; these will answer difficult questions that only the Bible will be able to answer. Proverbs 22:6 says: 'Choose the right path and when they are older, they will remain upon it.'

Even though parents are human and make mistakes, if we keep God's love and word in our hearts, He will give us the reassurance that we are 'godly' parents to our children. God cares for us that He gives us life, money and all we need for a living. So why worry?

CHAPTER TWELVE

ദോരു

WHY WORRY?

What a world so beautiful, so lovely, so enjoyable, so enticing and sweet! A world of joy and peace - of humility and loyalty! A world of love and care, of success and progress; a reasonable and understanding world! A pleasant world, a world made by God to be beautiful indeed!

Why killings? Why hatred? Why discrimination? Why sufferings? Why difficulties? Why challenges and problems? Why frustrations? Why sorrows? Why grief? Why greed? Why confusions and distractions? Why conflict and moral breakdowns? Life is afflicted with predicaments - why intimidations and fears?

Life is tempted to go astray! What a life of WORRY! Why worry when there is GOD? Why worry when you can overcome all challenges of life? Embrace challenges when they come, make them your friend and they will be gentle with you, they will be kind to you, then wisdom will help you to overcome.

Worrying is where one uncontrollably engages in chains of negative thought. It involves mental attempts to avoid anticipated potential threats. As an emotion, worrying is experienced as anxiety or a concern about a real or imagined issue. It is usually focused upon personal issues such as health and finances or broader ones such as environmental pollution and social or technological change. Most people who experience short-lived periods of worry may enjoy positive effects if they are prompted to take precautions or avoid risk.

I have spent an awful lot of time in my life worrying. I have worried about grades in school, job interviews, approaching deadlines and shrinking budgets. I have worried about bills and expenses, rising gas prices, insurance costs and endless taxes. I have worried about having my home in perfect condition for 'company', and within seconds of their arrival, the house is turned upside down and no one even noticed. I have worried about first impressions, political correctness, identity theft and contagious infections. In spite of all worrying, 'I'm still alive and well, and my bills are paid.' Said an American man.

Over the span of my lifetime, worrying accounts for hours and hours of invaluable time that I will never get back. So, I have decided that I would like to spend my time more wisely and more enjoyably. However, worry is a disease that causes suffering and kills man so easily. It destroys your being and takes you to an early grave. It is true to state that man breathes in worry as 'oxygen' and breathes it out as 'carbon dioxide.'

Man feeds on worry all day long; man is worrisome. God loves you so much that he made you in order to live but not to live by worrying. God so loved the world that he gave his only begotten Son, that whosoever believes in him shall not perish but have everlasting life - John 3:16.

When man is surrounded by worry, it deprives him of everlasting life. Only if you believe in His Son Jesus Christ will your life never perish by worrying.

My beloved! Why worry when God has given you life? Why worry when He thinks of you? Why worry when God provides for you?

Worry is the enemy of life because it destroys the mind and makes life short. Why worry?

PSALM 23

Psalm 23:1-6 reads: The Lord is my shepherd; I shall not want. He makes me to lie down in green pastures; he leads me beside the still waters. He restores my soul; he leads me in paths of righteousness for his name sake. Even though, I walk through the valley and shadow of death, I will fear no evil; for thou art with me, thy rod and thy staff, they comfort me. Thou preparest a table before me in the presence of my enemies; thou anointed my head with oil, my cup runs over. Surely goodness and mercy shall follow me all the days of my life; and I shall dwell in the house of the Lord forever. Amen!

Verse one of this chapter talked effectively on God's provisions. There's nothing we need in this life; food, money, health, wealth, shelter; name it, that God will not provide for us. If you are not convinced yet to give up your worrying, here are four biblical reasons not to worry.

1. **Worrying accomplishes absolutely nothing**: I do not know about you, but I don't have any time to waste these days. Worrying is a waste of very precious time. Worrying won't help or solve a problem or bring about a solution, so why waste your time and energy on it?

   Matthew 6:27-29: Can all your worries add a single moment to your life? And why worry about your clothing? Look at the lilies of the field and how they grow. They don't work or make their clothing, yet Solomon in all his glory was not dressed as beautifully as they are (NLT).

2. **Worrying is not good for you**: Worrying is destructive to us in many ways. It becomes a mental burden that can even cause us to grow physically sick.

   Proverbs 12:25: Worry weighs a person down; an encouraging word cheers a person up.

3. **Worrying is the opposite of trusting God**: The energy that we spend on worrying can be put to much better use in prayer. Here's a little formula to remember: worry replaced by prayer equals trust.

   Matthew 6:30: And if God cares so wonderfully for wild flowers that are here today and thrown into the fire tomorrow, He will certainly care for you. Why do you have so little faith? (NLT)

   Philippians 4:6-7: Don't worry about anything; instead, pray about everything, tell God what you need and thank him for what He has done. Then you will experience God's peace, which exceeds anything we can understand. His peace will guard your hearts and minds as you live in Christ Jesus. (NLT)

4. **Worrying puts your focus in the wrong direction**: When we keep our eyes focused on God, we remember His love for

us and we realise we truly have nothing to worry about. God has a wonderful plan for our lives and part of that plan includes taking care of us. Even in difficult times, when it seems like God doesn't care, we can put our trust in the Lord and focus on His kingdom. God will take care of our every need.

Matthew 6:25: That is why I tell you not to worry about everyday life – whether you have enough food, drink or enough clothes to wear. Isn't life more than food and your body more than clothing? (NLT)

Matthew 6:31-33: So don't worry about these things, saying: What will we eat? What will we drink? What will we wear? These things dominate the thoughts of unbelievers, but your heavenly father already knows all your needs. Seek the kingdom of God above all else, and live righteously, and he will give you everything you need.

1 Peter 5:7: Give all your worries and cares to God, for he cares about you.

Below are some useful quotations:

1.   'The problem of life is to change worry into thinking and anxiety into creative action.'
        Harold B. Walker

2. 'Worry is interest paid on trouble before it is due.' **William R. Inge**

3. 'Today is the tomorrow we worried about yesterday.' **Author Unknown**

4. 'It is not working that kills, but worry.' **African proverb**

5. 'Worry a little bit every day and in a lifetime you will lose a couple of years. If something is wrong, fix it if you can. But train yourself not to worry: worry never fixes anything.' **Ernest Hemingway**

6. 'What were you worried about this time last year - can't remember?' **Author unknown**

7. 'Don't worry, be happy.' **Bobby McFerrin**

8. 'Do not anticipate trouble or worry about what may never happen. Keep in the sunlight.' **Benjamin Franklin**

9. 'I've seen many troubles in my time only half of which ever came true.' **Mark Twain**

10. 'If you are distressed by anything external, the pain is not due to the thing itself but to

your own estimate of it and this you have no power to revoke at any moment.'
Charles F. Kettering

Conclusion

Dear friends, these quotations confirm that worry brings down your human nature with low self esteem.

CHAPTER THIRTEEN

ഇഇൻ

SELF ESTEEM

What is so significant about self esteem? It seems that every time you turn around, some TV psychologist is telling us how to feel about ourselves, our lives and our children. I don't know about you, but I had no idea I was supposed to be feeling so badly about myself.

Self esteem is a term that psychologists use to explain a person's feelings about themselves. When it comes to self esteem, its concern is widespread these days but it wasn't long ago when concerns of self esteem weren't around. These days, however, self esteem and the impulse to make sure positive self esteem is in our children seems to be the force to every experience we have.

Self esteem and violence

For some time, psychologists suggest that school bullies must suffer from low self esteem and are taking out their frustration by threatening and frightening other students. Yet, in 2001, a study assessed that self esteem in bullies was in fact the opposite. Children with excessively high esteem are more inclined to turn into bullies since they will not accept anyone else demeaning them in any capacity. This raised questions as to whether or not some schools go way too far when trying to prevent failure among children. One particular school in Massachusetts has even gone so far as to have jump-rope sessions without the ropes so as to prevent potential bad feelings caused by tripping over the rope. Hence adults, particularly males, are more prone to violent behaviour.

High but unstable self esteem

In most cases an unsafe combination is a very high, but unstable self esteem. What is obvious is that most violent criminals generally describe themselves as being better than anybody else. That is why trying to rationalise with them during an attack gets you nowhere. Non-lethal self defense guns are an ideal option in addition to being effective for you or your loved ones, when you should feel threatened by a person.

These days you can be stylish and safe when you acquire a pink-tazer or any one of the obtainable fashion colours. Relatively few attacks are crimes of passion; rather, they are crimes of opportunity. Knowing that you are able to defend yourself in many situations will increase your self esteem, but do it in a fashion that shows some common sense and justification. Learn to defend yourself so you can protect your very worthwhile self and stay safe.

I believe low self esteem and lack of confidence go hand in hand. When you don't feel good about the way you look, about the job you're in, how you handle finances or about your relationships and how you relate with others, you tend to ignore areas of your life causing you to miss out. Or as a female, you may have difficulty developing relationships with other females because you were jealous of the way they looked or dressed or what position they held.

Does this sound familiar? If you are like most women, then it probably does.

So, where does all this lack of self confidence come from? Often it stems from childhood or perhaps a bad relationship. Most often, the way someone else has treated us or words that were said once or a thousand times have been engrained into our minds.

For instance, with TV stars who appear to have perfect bodies; we are taught that we're supposed to look like them and if we don't, then no man will ever love us and we'll never get a good paying job.

I want you to know right now, that this is a lie from the pit of hell. Most of the women on TV and in the movies have personal trainers and nutritionists that regulate what they eat and when and how much they exercise.

I know most people generally cannot afford that lifestyle and the women you see on the covers of magazines are air-brushed and photo-shopped to look the way they do; not to mention all the bottoms and facelifts celebrities have these days. But even still, other people and the media are not the cause of our low self esteem or lack of confidence; they are not the root of the problem. The root is much deeper within ourselves and we can overcome these feelings. You can retrain your brain to think good thoughts about yourself no matter how low your self esteem is. You can learn not to be jealous of others and how to forgive yourself when you make mistakes. You can learn how to exude confidence and hold your head high and you can learn how to relate well to others no matter their social status or yours.

How do I do this - you're probably asking? Well, with the help of a life coach. A life coach can help you see why you are suffering from low self esteem, help you get to the root of it and help you overcome it. Start on the road to a confident new you and start living the life you've always dreamed of. Low self esteem has never helped anyone and it surely will not help you. It can drive you into depression, anger, fear and a poor quality of life.

The way you think about yourself is the determining factor of how you interact with others.

What are some examples of low esteem?

- You are afraid to converse with others for fear that what you say will not be accepted.

- You believe that you are not attractive.

- You choose something and it turns out to be the worst one.

- Nothing you do seems to go right. You believe that most people do not like you.

- You feel swallowed up in a whirlpool of frustration.

These are not all inclusive; just some of the common symptoms.

Let us discuss some of the origins of low self esteem

Low self esteem usually starts in childhood when children are made to believe that they are worthless. Their self confidence is eroded and they succumb to the idea that they can never achieve success in anything they do. This leaves a lot of low self esteem and resentment. If that was your experience, it is time you cut yourself loose from that mindset and start your self improvement. Start reading about the life of successful persons and you will soon discover that many of them had such low self esteem that they could not even complete an elementary education.

So you ask, 'What can I do?' The answer lies in changing your thoughts; it is actually what you think that is the problem. Understand that those behaviours listed above are thoughts; they are only aspects in your mind that you need improvement on. Do not let low self esteem ruin your life. Be determined to improve your self esteem and you are on your way to a better quality of life. It may seem easier said than done, but what you need to do is stop thinking that the world is against you. Get determined to achieve what you desire. Stop blaming other people for your misfortunes. The world is not your problem. The hard truth is that *you* are your problem. From this moment on, realise that you must begin the process of self esteem improvement. Think the right way and be determined to win and you will. Just remember that success never comes easily and that is why determination is the counterpart of desperation.

Often times, one gets to the brink of success and with just a little disappointment or setback, one loses heart and gives up too easily and too soon.

There is a story in the book: 'Think and Grow Rich' about a man who quit just three feet away from gold. This is a parable about the lesson of not quitting. Too many people give up but who knows what great things they might have achieved if only they had persevered a little longer. With low self esteem, your life could be rather boring.

Change your thinking and you will begin to see improvements in your life. Make a very special effort to be what you really want to be. You are the one in control of your life and you have to seriously decide either to remain in a miserable state of low self esteem or develop a high self esteem with good character and self image.

Many decide to override their low self esteem and improve their attitude; whatever it took; and they became some of the greatest people that ever lived.

Reprogram your thinking and control your state of mind. You must believe that you are worth much more than you think or you will remain at the foot of the ladder and never make an attempt to climb it.

Do not waste your life away with feelings of inadequacies. Instead, think of ways to go about improving your self esteem. Success is yours; just reach out and grasp it.

Now, here are ten steps to help you build your self-esteem.

1. Adapt the attitude that you are a responsible and dependable person. Others will respect you and come to you willingly.

2. Do things for others before they ask you and without waiting for recognition. In other words, do things spontaneously for others because you want to; don't wait until someone says you have to.

3. Freely contribute your opinions and suggestions with your family. You will feel better and your family will benefit.

4. Participate in the decision-making process at work, home and at civic clubs. When your actions show people that you make and carry out responsible decisions, they will respect you more for having done so.

5. Accept the mistakes you made for what they are. These are human errors and mistakes are part of being human. Learn from them and move on.

6. Focus on the 'why' of your actions rather than the 'what'. Look at the effort and energy you put into doing something and the reasons behind it rather than looking so much at what you do.

7. Become an expert at looking for the positive potential in yourself and others. By learning to tune in to yourself and others, you will become an expert on building closer, more trusting relationships.

8. Have confidence in your ability to make good judgments. As you start believing in yourself, others will, too.

9. Develop the habit of expecting positive things to happen; you will soon learn that they will; even when disappointments first set in.

10. Look at different ways of seeing a situation. Use your creative abilities and look beyond the first right answer. Self esteem is having the 'I CAN' attitude.

CHAPTER FOURTEEN

ŞƆCȜ

GRATITUDE

Gratitude (thankfulness or appreciation) is a positive emotion or attitude in acknowledgement of a benefit one has received. Gratitude is an emotion that occurs after people receive help, depending on how they interpret the situation.

Specifically, gratitude is experienced if people perceive the help they receive as:

(a) Valuable to them
(b) Costly to their benefactor and
(c) Given by the benefactor with benevolent intentions (rather than ulterior motives.)

When faced with identical situations where they have been given help, different people view the situation very differently in terms of value, cost, and benevolent intentions. This explains why people feel differing levels of gratitude after they have been helped. People who generally experience more gratitude in life habitually interpret help as more costly, more beneficial and more beneficially intended, and this habitual bias explains why some people experience more gratitude than others.

Gratitude and indebtedness

Gratitude is not the same as indebtedness. While both emotions occur following help, indebtedness occurs when a person perceives that they are under an obligation to make some repayment or compensation for the aid. The emotions lead to different actions; indebtedness motivates the recipient to see out their benefactor and to improve their relationship with them.

Gratitude as a motivator of behaviour

Gratitude may also serve to reinforce future pro-social behaviour in benefactors. For example, one experiment found that customers of a jewelry store who were called and thanked showed a subsequent 70% increase in purchases. In comparison, customers who were thanked and told about a sale showed only a 30% increase in purchases, and customers who were not called at all did not show an increase. In another study, regular patrons of a restaurant gave bigger tips when servers wrote, 'Thank you' on their checks.

Major theoretical approaches to gratitude

The link between spirituality and gratitude has recently become a popular subject of study. While these two characteristics are certainly not dependent on each other, studies have found that spirituality is capable of enhancing a person's ability to be grateful and therefore, those who regularly attend religious services or engage in religious activities are more likely to have a greater sense of gratitude in all areas of life.

Gratitude is viewed as a prized human propensity in the Christian, Buddhist, Muslim, Jewish and Hindu traditions. Worship with gratitude to God is a common theme in such religions and therefore, the concept of gratitude permeates religious texts, teachings, and traditions. For this reason, it is one of the most common emotions that religions aim to provoke and maintain in followers and is regarded as a universal religious sentiment.

Hebraic conceptions of gratitude

In Judaism, gratitude is an essential part of the act of worship and a part of every aspect of a worshipper's life. According to Hebrews worldwide, all things come from God and because of this, gratitude is extremely important to the followers of Judaism. The Hebrew Scriptures are filled with the ideas of gratitude. Two examples included in the Psalms are 'O Lord my God, I will give thanks to you forever' and 'I will give thanks to the Lord with my whole heart'. (Ps. 30:12, 9:1) The Jewish prayers also often incorporate gratitude beginning with the Shema, where the worshipper states that out of gratitude you shall love the Eternal your God, with all your heart, with all your soul and with all your might. (Deut.6:5).

The concluding prayer, the Alenu, also speaks of gratitude by thanking God for the particular destiny of the Jewish people. Along with these prayers, faithful worshippers recite more than one hundred blessings called breakouts throughout the day.

Christian conceptions of gratitude

Gratitude has been said to mould and shape the entire Christian life. Christian reformists like Martin Luther, referred to gratitude as 'The basic Christian attitude' and today is still referred to as 'The heart of the gospel.'

As each Christian believes creation by a personal God, they are strongly encouraged to praise and give gratitude to their creator. In Christian gratitude, God is seen as the selfless giver of all good things and because of this, there is a great sense of indebtedness that enables Christians to share a common bond, shaping all aspects of a follower's life. Gratitude in Christianity is an acknowledgement of God's generosity that inspires Christians to shape their own thoughts and actions around such ideals. Instead of simply sentimental feelings, Christian gratitude is regarded as a virtue that shapes not only emotions and thoughts but actions and deeds as well. According to 17th century revivalist preacher and theologian, Jonathan Edwards; in his treatise concerning religious affections; love, gratitude and thankfulness towards God are among the signs of true religion. Because of this interpretation, modern measures of religious spirituality include assessments of thankfulness and gratitude towards God.

Allport (1950) suggested that mature religious intentions come from feelings of profound gratitude and Edwards (1746-1959) claimed that the 'affection' of gratitude is one of the most accurate ways of finding the presence of God in a person's life. In a study done by Samuels and Lester (1985) it was contended that in a small sample of catholic nuns and priests, out of fifty emotions, love and gratitude were the most experienced emotion towards God.

Islamic conceptions of gratitude

The Islamic holy book, the Koran, is filled with ideas of gratitude. Similar to the traditions of Judaism and Christianity, Islam encourages its followers to be grateful and express thanks to God in all circumstances. Islamic saying states that, 'The first who will be summoned to paradise are those who have praised God in every circumstance.'

In the Koran it also states in Sura 14 that those who are grateful will be given more by God. The prophet Mohammad also said, 'Gratitude for the abundance you have received is the best insurance that the abundance will continue.' Many essential practices of the Islamic faith also encourage gratitude. The pillar of Islam calling for daily prayer encourages believers to pray to God five times a day in order to thank Him for His goodness. The pillar of fasting during the month of Ramadan is for the purpose of putting the believers in a state of gratitude.

Individual differences in gratitude

Much of the recent psychological research into gratitude has focused on the nature of individual difference in gratitude and the conscquences of being a more or less grateful person.

Three scales measure eight different conceptions

The GQ6 measures individual differences in how frequently and intensely people experience gratitude. The appreciation scale measures eight different aspects of gratitude: appreciation of people, possessions and the present moment, rituals, feeling of awe, social comparisons, existential concerns and behaviour which expresses gratitude. The GRAT assesses gratitude towards other people, towards the world in general and a lack of resentment for what you do not have. A recent study showed that each of these scales is actually measuring the same way of approaching life. This suggests that individual differences in gratitude include all of these components: empirical findings, gratitude and well-being.

A large body of recent work has suggested that people who are more grateful have higher levels of well-being. Grateful people are happier, less depressed, less stressed and more satisfied with their lives and social relationships. Grateful people also have higher levels of control of their environments, personal growth, purpose in life and self acceptance.

Grateful people have more positive ways of coping with the difficulties they experience in life and are more likely to seek more time planning how to deal with the problem. Grateful people also have less negative coping strategies, being less likely to try to avoid the problem, deny that there is a problem, blame themselves, or cope through substance use. Grateful people sleep better and this seems to be because they think less negative and more positive thoughts just before going to bed. Gratitude has been said to have one of the strongest links with mental health of any character trait. Numerous studies suggest that grateful people are more likely to have higher levels of happiness and lower levels of stress and depression.

In one study concerning gratitude, participants were randomly assigned to one of the six therapeutic intervention conditions designed to improve the participant's overall quality of life (Seligman et. al, 2005). Out of these conditions, it was found that the biggest short-term effects came from a 'gratitude visit' where participants wrote and delivered a letter of gratitude to someone in their life. This condition showed a rise in happiness scores by 10 percent and a significant fall in depression scores; results which lasted up to one month after the visit. Out of the six conditions, the longest lasting effects were caused by the act of writing 'gratitude journals' where happiness scores of participants increased and continued to increase each time they were tested periodically after the experiment.

In fact, the greatest benefits were usually found to occur around six months after treatment began. This exercise was so successful that although participants were only asked to continue the journal for a week, many participants continued to keep the journal long after the study was over.

Similar results have been found from studies conducted by Emmons and McCullough (2003) and Lyubormirsky et al. (2005). Whilst many emotions and personality traits are important to well-being, there is evidence that gratitude may be uniquely important.

First, a longitudinal study showed that people who were more grateful coped better with a life transition. Specifically, people who were more grateful before the transitions were less stressed, less depressed and more satisfied with their relationship three months later. Second, two recent studies have suggested that gratitude may have a unique relationship with well-being and can explain aspects of well-being that other personality traits cannot. Both studies showed that gratitude has been able to explain more well-being than the 'Big five and thirty' of the most commonly studied personality traits.

Gratitude has been shown to improve a person's altruistic tendencies. One study conducted by David DeSteno and Monica Bartiett (2010) found that gratitude is correlated with economic generosity. In this study, using an economic game, increased gratitude was shown to directly mediate increased monetary giving. From these results, this study shows that gracious people are more likely to sacrifice individual gains for communal profit (DeSteno & Bartiett, 2010).

A study conducted by McCullough, Emmons & Tsang, (2002) found similar correlations between gratitude and empathy as well as generosity and helpfulness.

Given that gratitude appears to be a strong determinant of people's well-being, several psychological interventions have been developed to increase gratitude. For example, Watkins and colleagues got participants to test a number of different exercises, such as thinking about a living person to whom they were grateful, writing about someone to whom they were grateful and writing a letter to deliver to someone to whom they were grateful. This effect was strongest for participants who were asked to think about a person to whom they were grateful. Participants who had grateful personalities to begin with showed the greatest benefit from these gratitude exercises.

Conclusion

According to Cicero, 'Gratitude is only the greatest of the virtues but the parent of all others.' Multiple studies have shown the correlation between gratitude and increased well-being not only for the individual but for all people involved. The positive psychology movement has embraced these studies and in an effort to increase overall well-being, has begun to make an effort to incorporate exercises to increase gratitude into the movement. Although gratitude has been neglected by psychology in the past, in recent years, much progress has been made in studying gratitude and its positive effects.

'I love to write, I love to sing, I love to dance, I love to preach the gospel of God and I love to run because it's in me.' Do that which is in you.

CHAPTER FIFTEEN

MAXIMISING YOUR POTENTIAL

Potential is the God-given abilities, skills and talents we have. Specifically, skills we use fall into three categories which I borrowed from Richard Nelson Bolles' book: *What colour is your parachute?* These skills are used with:

1. people
2. information
3. things

1. With people, we use thirteen basic skills:

   (a) Speaking or listening to others so as to convey or receive information (communicating.)

   (b) Influencing others by our words or actions (persuading.)

   (c) Showing sensitivity to the feelings of others (serving.)

   (d) Caring for others by using specified techniques or approaches to improve their physical, mental, emotional or spiritual problem (treating.)

(e) Giving expert advice or giving relevant recommendations based on our own area of expertise (advising.)

(f) Paying attention to instructions and then carrying out the prescribed action (taking instructions.)

(g) Monitoring behaviour and coordinating it in order to achieve organisational objectives (managing/supervising.)

(h) Recognising and utilising the skills of others (leading.)

(i) Arriving at an individual or jointly agreed upon decision usually through discussion and compromise (negotiating/deciding.)

(j) Exhibiting showmanship for fun, laughter or entertainment (entertaining or amusing.)

(k) Dealing with the problems of others in the context of their total self while helping them to identify and receive them through self-directed action (counseling.)

(l) Giving new information or ideas to people through lecture, demonstration or practice (training.)

2. With information, we use our skills in fourteen different ways:

    (a) We investigate, detect, compile and classify information by means of research (researching.)

    (b) We examine two or more people or objects in order to learn about and react to their similarities and dissimilarities (comparing.)

    (c) We study the behaviour of people, animals, or things or the details of a particular phenomenon or place (observing.)

    (d) We perceive and define cause and effect relations (analysing.)

    (e) We deal with numbers in performing complex arithmetic (computing.)

    (f) We give a definite structure and working order to things (organising.)

    (g) We inspect, diagnose, test and evaluate information, people or things (evaluating.)

    (h) We take what others have developed and apply it to new situations often in a new cohesive whole (creating.)

(i)   We fashion or shape things (designing.)

(j)   We conceive shapes or sounds by perceiving their patterns and structures and we enable others to see them, too (visualising.)

(k)   We record, memorise or reproduce on paper or in the mind (copying, storing, and retrieving.)

(l)   We determine the sequence of tasks after reviewing pertinent data or requirements (planning, developing.)

(m)   We systematically accomplish tasks in a manner that causes objectives to be attained or surpassed (achieving.)

(n)   We speed up the accomplishment of a task or series of tasks so as to reach an organisational objective on or ahead of time (expediting.)

3. Finally, let's look at the skills we use with things:

(a)   Using our body as an instrument of accomplishment (being athletic.)

(b)   Using our hands or body to identify or move an object (handling.)

(c)   Manipulating hand tools (using tools.)

(d)   Monitoring, adjusting and servicing automatic machines (minding machines, operating machines or equipment.)

(e)   Performing some or all operations upon a vehicle (operating a vehicle.)

(f)   Using earth as an instrument of accomplishment (working with nature.)

(g)   Preparing, building, installing and displaying machinery (setting up displays, machinery or equipment.)

(h)   Attaining precise set of limits, tolerance or standards (precision working).

(i)   Putting an object back into good working condition or similar to its original condition (preparing.)

I encourage you to make an inventory of the skills that have brought you success and satisfaction. Then look for creative ways to emphasise them. When you do, you'll be maximising your potential. Beginning today, don't wait for anyone to make you feel good. Become your own best friend.

<u>Here are three steps to help you get started</u>:

1.   Look inside yourself to see what gives you the most satisfaction and go for it.

2. Become familiar with the people and places where you feel respected and valued.

3. Learn to encourage yourself. Make it a natural habit. When you don't value yourself as a person, you may not be able to recognise all your strengths. When you begin to encourage yourself, you'll become more satisfied with your life. As you begin to recognise and value your strengths and resources, you will start to give yourself more positive messages.

As you become more satisfied, you will not feel a need to compare yourself with others. Instead, you will note your own progress and set your own standards. You'll feel like working with people, not against them.

FIVE RESOLUTIONS FOR MAXIMISING YOUR POTENTIAL

1. **Quit Tolerating:** To attract new and better opportunities and results, first clear out what's clogging up your life and create space for improvements. List the things that you tolerate which limit productivity, cause stress and waste time and energy. Then determine what needs to happen to

eliminate these problem areas. If you no longer accept being dragged down by unwelcome events, problems or the behaviour of others, you will stop wasting time managing these unnecessary and unwanted situations.

2. **Play your Game**: The best game to play is one where you make up your own rules. If you encounter resistance in reaching some goals, chances are it's either something you really don't want to be doing, an old goal that may no longer serve you or a part of someone else's agenda. Take the time to discover what you truly want by aligning your goals with the priorities in your life rather than with the 'shields.'

3. **Creating a winning routine**: Are you busy with tasks that consume you and your schedule? Do you feel that you're fighting the clock? Design a weekly routine that complements your goals and focus on those activities that support your objectives and enhance your lifestyle. This includes planning for the unplanned as well. Make time your ally instead of your adversary by under-promising on your personal and professional deadlines. Develop a highly

effective routine, get organised, eliminate distractions, reduce stress and manage your tasks in order to reach and exceed your goals.

4. **Deepen your learning**: While we attract what we need to learn, we often resist the lessons. If similar problems keep reappearing, we have obviously missed the lesson. To accelerate success, take a lesson from every experience and person and write it down in order to grow and progress onto a new and improved path.

5. **Expand your vision**: What does your ideal life look like? The fact is, we never grow past what we feel is possible. Let go of your current perceptions that inhibit your ability to explore greater possibilities and achieve more. Clarify what success looks like in every area of your life career, relationship, health, environment, etc. It's a lot easier to create something great when you know exactly what you're looking for. Besides, it's your canvass. What masterpiece do you want to create?

DEFINION OF TERMS

Challenge: The act of making something different in every way.

Fate: The bad things that have happened to somebody – internally, externally and otherwise.

Disability: A state by which one cannot or is not able to use any part of the body completely or easily.

God: The creator of the universe, the preserve of man and the world; the redeemer and judge of all.

Parent: A father or mother; one who is exercising the function of a father or a mother.

Father: A male who has begotten a child and cares for the child.

Care: A process of showing concern, regard or interest in a person. It is the act of watching over somebody or paying attention to someone. Here, the father makes an adequate provision for whatever the child needs.

APPENDAGES

MY QUOTES

1. Life is like a good seed planted in the garden and covered with a heap of sand. As the seed germinates from the ground, so shall every soul buried arise from the dead on the day of resurrection.

2. Until you're tried, you will not come out as gold. Trial produces triumph.

3. You cannot be yourself until you deposit that which is in you - i.e. - your potential and skills. You are never born empty.

4. As a candle is lighted and waxes in a moment, so shall a man born of a woman live for a short moment and die.

5. I love to write; I love to sing. I love to dance, I love to preach; I love to run because it's in me. Do that which is in you.

6. The mindset of a man is the bed rock of his life. As he thinks, so is he. (Proverbs.23:7)

7. A desire to achieve is better than a dream without a vision.

8.   As the day gives birth to another day by passing through the night, so shall your dreams give birth to achievements by passing through determination.

9.   Get ready for the coming of tomorrow; it can come with good or with bad. All hope is in God Almighty.

10.   You cannot live unless you are born, you cannot be born unless you are conceived and you cannot be conceived unless both parents are productive. Think about it.

11.   If you think you're free of life's challenges, you have reasons to give. No one is born with a symbol of perfection.

12.   Life is a place of study; it has its book and it teaches its lessons according to an individual's experience.

13.   Success is the 'honeymoon' of a fulfilled dream. Live to achieve success.

14.   Greatness is not by your intellect; it is your mindset.

15.   Forgiveness is the art of the mind; it conquers sin, buys love and brings life to its fulfillments.

16.   Forgiveness is compassionate; it gives the mind a better shape and nourishes the body with love for a healthy living.

17. Forgiveness is like an animal you killed to eat. After killing it, you realise you are the animal – forgiveness tears the mind of agony and kills the body, spirit and soul of hatred. Unless you forgive you can never be yourself.

18. Forgiveness is like a home. In the home there is love, peace of mind, joy and understanding of oneself. There is humility and tolerance. As you forgive, you create a home to everyone that offends you.

19. I cannot forgive you unless you offend me; you cannot offend me unless you know me; you cannot know me unless we come across each other. Offence is part of life, forgiveness is part of life, knowing is part of life - all is vital to life.

20. For you to forgive, you have to obtain forgiveness from someone you offended so that it can give you the zeal to forgive others.

21. Offence is the arm of life. It makes life blue and destroys the image of living. It neutralises forgiveness which makes man complete.

22. The purpose of living is to forgive. If you cannot forgive, then you cannot live. Remember you only hurt yourself more when you do not forgive. Be wise.

23. Men of honour, men of integrity, men of humility and men of right attitude are rare but are worthy of relationship and high esteem.

24. The integrity of a man determines his quality of living.

25. Moderation is the mother of long life.

26. The values you press on and the morals you possess measure the integrity in you.

27. Life is true living. Live to fulfill your destiny.

28. Ignorance is a disease; it disapproves man and deprives him of knowledge.

29. Love is a tree planted in a fertile land; it grows with time but needs nourishment. It's in you - build your love for others.

30. Love is a powerful key that strengthens relationships. True love covers faults and does not fail. It sticks till the end.

31. The dream of success is a difficult thing to achieve; it needs your in-built power, hard work and determination.

32. Real gifts don't depend on quantity but on quality no matter how small. Some gifts speak volume.

33. Appearance tells the physical shape of man. 'He is the richest whose pleasures are cheapest.'

34. Good attitude renews your youth.

35. Worry is the enemy of life because it destroys the mind and makes life short. Why worry?

36. The survival of a man depends on his fitness. Background is not the only answer to survival. Think about it.

37. Life is all about relationships. Relate well and enjoy life.

38. The inward beauty of a woman gives way to her greatness, virtuousness and gloriousness.

39. Hard work is the answer to wealthy living.

40. There is no limit to where your potential, gifts and skills can take you except the limit you create for yourself. Think about it.

41. You are at your best when you operate to the standard of your potential.

42. Think of living. Think of dying. Which one is more important?

43.	That which frustrates and causes contemporaries to break down in your life is the same that will inspire you to break records.

44.	Asking for forgiveness is deriding to man but it is the best way to live by love. Ask and you shall receive.

45.	A new day comes with a new appearance and new attitude to man. How he welcomes it gives him an answer to his purpose for the day.

46.	A fool is one who deposits his life to worry and banks with fear and anger. 'By prayer, make your request known to God.' (Philippians 4:6)

47.	Money makes a man and creates a better living for him but the love of it brings ruin.

48.	The painful stage in life is when you are suffering to earn a living. But do all things with joy and passion.

49.	Your destiny is in your hands to let it die or make it live. Choose.

50.	No matter the present difficulties of life, with endurance and faith in God, you shall become that which God has purposely made you to be.

51. Boldness is the act of the mind - it beats off fear and plants courage in the heart of man.

52. Socialism, love and cheerfulness are the powers to overcome hatred.

53. Men of inspiration are men of integrity and intellect. They have burning desires to achieve their goals.

54. Writers never stop writing until writing ends.

55. Growth is a maximum effort every individual must aspire to achieve because it keeps you living.

56. Growth is like an invisible ripe fruit on the way of everyone; unless you have the keys, you cannot pluck it.

57. Growth is beyond height; it is physical, mental and spiritual. Grab all and enjoy your living.

58. If you cannot grow, do not live because you must grow if you live.

59. Growth is not acquired by power or by one's

strength but rather by prayer, focus, maximum effort, determination and vision.

60. Aspire to grow, dream to grow, be determined to grow and pray to grow. But make sure to grow in a homely order because life is all about focus.

61. Speak of that which seems impossible; believe it is possible, and then you will conquer.

62. Moments of challenges are moment of blues; only your faith will see you through.

63. Challenges make men strong in spirit and believe there is God.

64. I know myself more than you know me but God knows me more than I know myself.

65. I strongly believe in what I can do and in what God can do through me to influence my generation.

66. Life ends in remembrance. Do something good which you will be remembered by.

67. Opportunities are like fallen flowers which can never climb again, so grab every good opportunity that you come across and you will prosper.

68.   Man has two leading lives - normal life and secret life.

69.   Money is a thing to earn, a thing to acquire and a thing to work for but go for it in a righteous way.

70.   Do well to people while still alive for a day shall come when you shall need someone who will do well for you.

LOOK OUT FOR BLESSING AGBAKWURU'S

NEXT BOOK:

'BORN TO BE GREAT'